ANIMAL TRACKERS

BY THE SEASHORE

Tessa Paul

 CRABTREE
Publishing Company

CRABTREE
Publishing Company

350 Fifth Avenue
Suite 3308
New York, NY 10118

360 York Road, R.R.4
Niagara-on-the-Lake
Ontario L0S 1J0

73 Lime Walk
Headington, Oxford
England OX3 7AD

Editor **Bobbie Kalman**
Assistant Editor **Virginia Mainprize**
Designers **Emma Humphreys-Davies Richard Shiner Melissa Stokes**

Illustrations by

Front Cover: Fiona Currie; Introduction: Andrew Beckett, Rod Sutterby; Andrew Beckett (p.24, 27), Robin Bouttelle/WLAA (p.22 – 23), Wendy Bramail/WLAA (p.14), Joanne Cowne (p.6 –7, 26 – 27), John Cox/WLAA (p.24 – 25), Barry Croucher/WLAA (p.20 – 21), Guy Croucher/WLAA (p.18), Ruth Grewcock (p.18 – 19), Angela Hargreaves/WLAA (p.28), Phillip Hood/WLAA (p.8 – 9), Terence Lambert (p.16 – 17), Gareth Llewhellin/WLAA (p.14 – 15), Dave Mead (p.13), Robert Moton (p.12), Deborah Pulley/WLAA (p.6), David Scott/WLAA (p.30 – 31), Chris Shields/WLAA (p.28 – 29), Guy Troughton (p.20), Simon Turvey/WLAA (p.10 – 11, 24); all track marks by Andrew Beckett

First printed 1997
Copyright © 1997 Marshall Cavendish Ltd.

Cataloging-in-Publication Data

Paul, Tessa
By the seashore / Tessa Paul
p. cm. – – (Animal trackers)
Includes index.
Summary: Introduces such seashore animals as the sandpiper, sea turtle, and crab.
ISBN 0-86505-587-4 (RLB) – – ISBN 0-86505-595-5 (paper)
1. Seashore animals – Juvenile literature   [1. Seashore animals.]
I. Title.   II. Series: Paul, Tessa . Animal trackers .
QL122.2.P38 1997   591.769"9– – dc21   96-45707   CIP AC

Printed and bound in Malaysia

CONTENTS

INTRODUCTION

When you walk on the beach, all you may see at first is water and sand. However, there are animals all around you. Tiny crabs rest in rock pools. Birds sit on high rocks or float on the water, ready to dive for fish. Turtle eggs are buried in the sand. What tracks do these animals leave?

There are many signs of animal life. The back of a whale rises out of the water. Cormorant nests are on the

ground. Fur seals crowd bays. Foxes leave bones and feathers on the beach after they have eaten.

This book is filled with colorful pictures. They show you animals which live on the shore or spend their lives in the sea. You will find out where to see these animals and birds. You will discover the best season for finding these sea creatures.

This book also tells you what to listen for when you are on the beach. Whales slap the water with their huge tails. Some birds screech, others croak, others make little piping noises. Otters and seals bark. Soon, you will learn that the sea is not only waves and sand.

GRAY WHALE

Gray whales spend their lives travelling. In spring, they migrate up the west coast of North America to the seas around Alaska. There, they spend the summer, eating tons of tiny sea creatures. In the autumn, they swim 5,000 miles back south. Gray whales then spend the winter in the warm waters off the coast of Mexico.

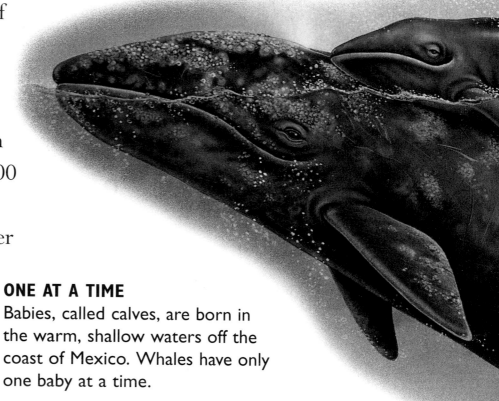

ONE AT A TIME
Babies, called calves, are born in the warm, shallow waters off the coast of Mexico. Whales have only one baby at a time.

GRAY WHALE

HUMPBACK WHALE

KILLER WHALE

DORSAL FINS
Some sea animals swim close to the surface. You can see their backs above the water. Killer whales have a sharp, pointed fin. Humpbacked whales have a low, curved fin. Gray whales do not have a dorsal fin, but have a round, bumpy back.

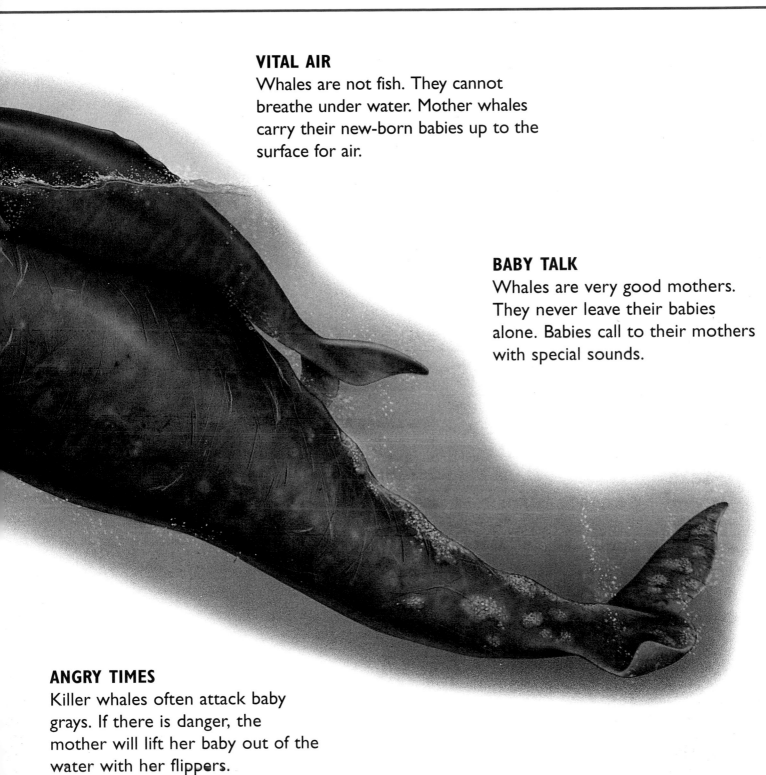

VITAL AIR
Whales are not fish. They cannot breathe under water. Mother whales carry their new-born babies up to the surface for air.

BABY TALK
Whales are very good mothers. They never leave their babies alone. Babies call to their mothers with special sounds.

ANGRY TIMES
Killer whales often attack baby grays. If there is danger, the mother will lift her baby out of the water with her flippers.

When whales travel close to shore, you can watch them. Many signs show where the whales are swimming. You may spot their huge, round backs sticking out of the water. You will see when whales come to the surface to breathe out air. High spouts of air spray out of the whales with a loud whooshing sound. You may also see whales jumping out of the water. They flap their huge tails called flukes.

SNACK TIME
These huge animals eat tiny shrimp called krill. They catch millions at a time in their enormous mouth.

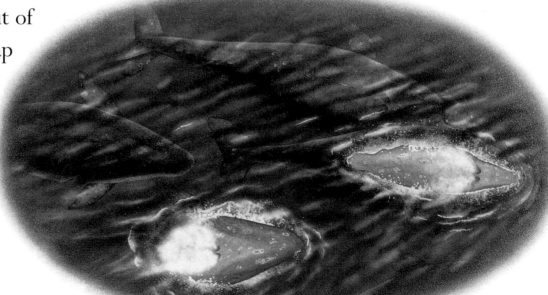

WHAT A SIGHT
Gray whales travel together in large groups called gams. You may see their giant bodies moving under the water.

JUST CHECKING
Grays will lift their heads out of the water and take a look around. This is called spy-hopping.

SANDPIPER

There are more than ninety different types of sandpipers. They live all over the world. During the spring and part of the summer, the upland sandpiper is found in many parts of Canada and the United States. You will recognize it because of its straight bill, long tail, small head, and slim legs. However, sitting on its nest, it is completely camouflaged.

HOME FLIGHT
When sandpipers fly over their nesting grounds, they curve their wings down. As they land, they lift their wings for a moment, fold them down, and close them.

SHARED WORK
The nest, built on the ground, is hidden in the grass. It is difficult to see. Sandpipers lay four pinkish-brown eggs. Both parents sit on the nest. The new-born chicks leave the nest as soon as they are born.

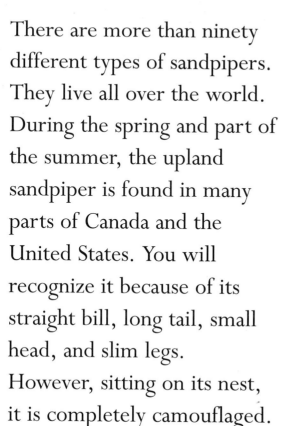

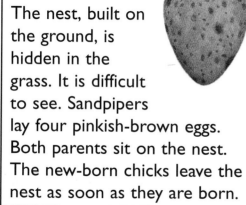

LITTLE WEBS
The toes are webbed only at the base.

NORTH TO SOUTH

Upland sandpipers spend the summer in Canada and the United States. Each August, as soon as the young can fly, they migrate. They travel thousands of miles to the grassy plains of South America.

11

SEA TURTLE

Not all sea turtles have a hard shell, or carapace. Leatherbacks have tough, thick skin that looks like a shell. The leatherback swims along the east and west coasts of Canada. Sea turtles with hard shells prefer warm water. They are found in warm seas all over the world.

RECORD SWIMMERS
Sea turtles can swim a very long way. They have been known to swim 1,000 miles across the Atlantic Ocean.

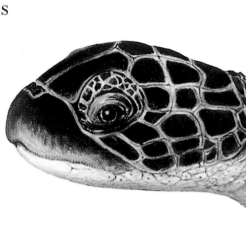
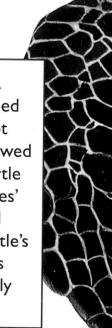

TORTOISE SHELL AND PAW

LAND AND SEA
Land turtles are called tortoises and do not swim. They have clawed feet, but the sea turtle has flippers. Tortoises' shells are rough and domed. The sea turtle's shell is smooth. This helps it to glide easily through the water.

RISKY BUSINESS
All turtles bury their eggs. The female digs a hole, then lays up to two hundred rubbery eggs. Many are eaten by crabs, birds, and other animals.

PERFECT FOR PADDLING
The back legs of the sea turtle are short and broad. They are paddle-shaped flippers that give the animal speed and strength in the water.

PUFFIN

Puffins nest in colonies. They come together in large groups to lay their eggs and raise their chicks. If you visit a puffin colony, you will see thousands of puffins standing together on rocky cliffs or diving into the ocean. After the breeding season, puffins return to the sea.

TAKING-OFF

Taking off from the water is hard for puffins. They splash over the surface, beating their wings up and down. When they dive down into the sea from their high cliffs, they fold their wings close to their body.

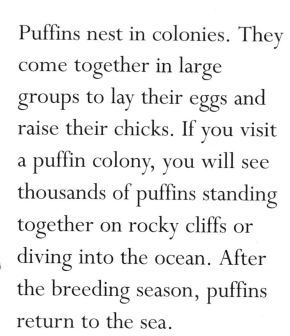

COLOR CHANGES

Because they have large, colored bills, puffins are called "sea parrots." In the summer, puffins are easy to see. Their feathers are pure white and shiny black. Their feet are red, and their large, thick bills are red, blue, and yellow. In the winter, the feathers turn dull, and the bill is smaller and paler.

NIMBLE BIRDS

Puffins walk along narrow ledges and jump from rock to rock. They stand up on their toes. They call each other with purrs and croaks.

ALL AT SEA

Puffins use their wings to swim under water. They use their webbed feet as rudders. They dive deep, chasing after small fish.

IN THE NEST

Puffins dig a burrow in the ground for their nest. Father and mother take turns sitting on their single, white egg. When the chick hatches, both parents bring it fish.

SEAL

Fur seals live in the North Pacific Ocean. They are excellent swimmers and spend most of their life at sea. During the day, they rest on the waves, floating along on the ocean currents. You may see one, with a flipper waving in the air, as it swims lazily off shore. At night, they hunt, diving deep under the water to catch fish. Summer after summer, they return to the rocky coast to have their babies. Each winter, mother seals, called cows, and their babies, called pups, travel down the coast to warmer waters.

LAYERS OF WARMTH

These seals have a top layer of long guard hairs. Underneath is a thick coat of shorter hair. Under the skin is a thick layer of fat called blubber. This gives the seal extra warmth.

WHAT WHISKERS!

Young seals have long, brown whiskers. These turn white as the animal gets older. The whiskers are like feelers and help seals find food.

DEEP SEA FISHING

Webbed flippers and a long, streamlined body make seals excellent swimmers. They dive after fish and catch them in their mouth.

A SEA NOSE

Like all mammals, seals breathe in the air, not in water. When they dive, their narrow nostrils close.

Fur seals live alone much of the year. But, in the breeding season, large colonies form. You can see thousands of seals gathered together along rocky shores where they will have their babies. The males, called bulls, bark and fight as they find female partners. They make so much noise you can hear them from afar.

FLIP-FLOPS
When they swim, seals use their front flippers as paddles. They steer with their back flippers. On land, they use their flippers to crawl over the rocks.

BEACH MASTER
Each male lives with a group of females called a harem. The younger males, who are not strong enough to win the fight for females, move away.

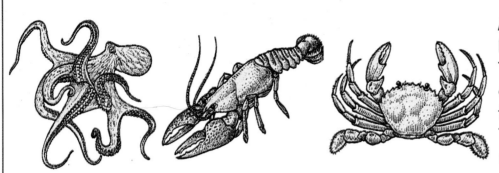

A FISHY DIET

Fur seals are carnivores. This means they eat other animals. They catch fish, squid, and shellfish. They also catch sea birds nesting on the ground.

MAMA'S GONE A-HUNTING

Mothers nurse their pups for a week after birth. Then, they go hunting, returning every few days to feed their young.

BRANT GOOSE

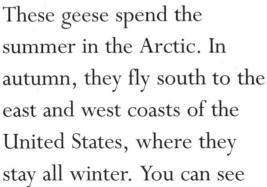

These geese spend the summer in the Arctic. In autumn, they fly south to the east and west coasts of the United States, where they stay all winter. You can see them flying in large flocks or long, thin lines.

SOUND EFFECTS

Brant geese do not honk like Canada geese. They call to each other in deep grunts and hoarse croaks. They make chattering sounds when they eat.

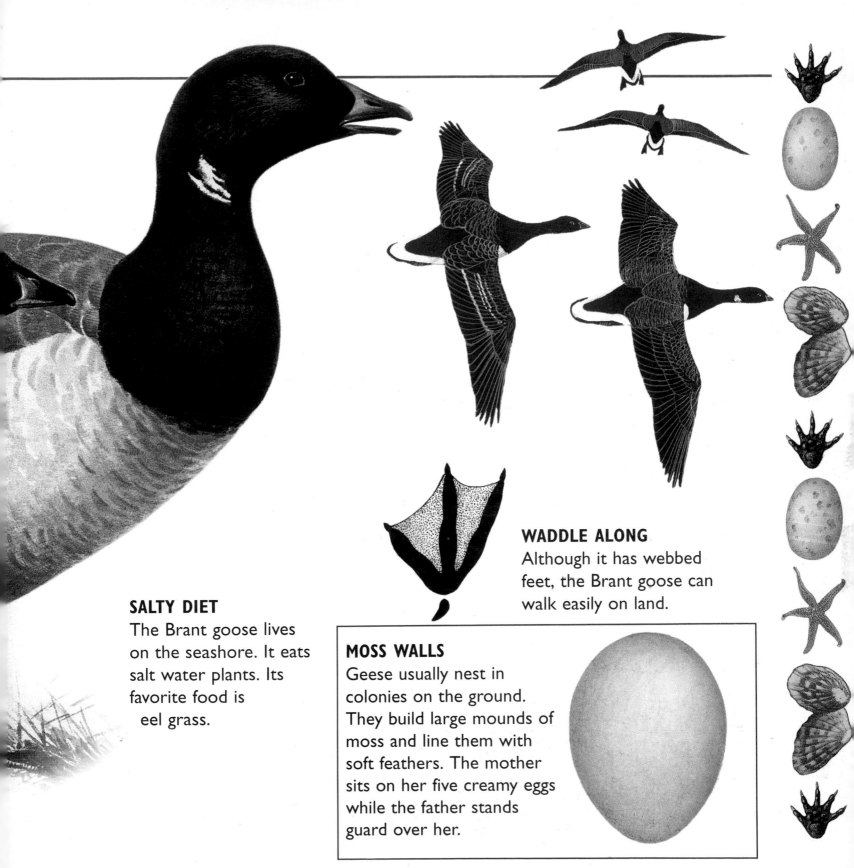

SALTY DIET
The Brant goose lives on the seashore. It eats salt water plants. Its favorite food is eel grass.

WADDLE ALONG
Although it has webbed feet, the Brant goose can walk easily on land.

MOSS WALLS
Geese usually nest in colonies on the ground. They build large mounds of moss and line them with soft feathers. The mother sits on her five creamy eggs while the father stands guard over her.

ARCTIC FOX

The Arctic fox lives in northern Canada. It is hard to spot because it is well camouflaged and blends in with the landscape. In the winter, its fur turns white like snow. In the summer, it sheds its winter coat, and its fur is brown.

NOT PICKY
Arctic foxes are carnivores, hunting small animals and stealing birds and eggs from ground nests. They are also scavengers, happy to eat the leftovers found from another animal's meal.

WARM TOES
Fox tracks look very like dog prints. The soles of their feet are covered with fur.

A STRONG HOME
Year after year, foxes return to the same den. Many tunnels lead down into it. Bones, feathers, and shells mark the entrances.

CORMORANT

The cormorant floats on the waves, looking for food under the water. When it sees a fish, it dives straight down and catches it. The cormorant comes out of the sea, holding the fish in its mouth. It tosses the fish in the air, then swallows it whole.

WING DRYING

You can easily spot the cormorant. It stands for hours with its wings stretched, drying the feathers. This bird spends a lot of its life in water, yet it does not have waterproof feathers!

SEA VIEWS

Cormorants have stick nests, lined with seaweed. They build in trees or on cliffs over the sea. Their four eggs are pale blue. Both parents feed the chicks.

WATER WEBS
Webbed feet make them excellent swimmers and deep divers.

DEEP TALK
Cormorants live in colonies near water. They make deep grunting sounds.

FEATHERS
Young birds are not as dark as the older ones. Their underparts are pale brown. Both young and old have hooked bills.

CRAB

Some crabs are tiny. Others have bodies more than a foot across. Some have big claws, strong enough to take off a finger. Because so many animals eat them, crabs are often in danger. When the tide goes out, crabs run and hide in tidal pools.

SEA BEADS

The pea crab is so round it looks like a bead. The males are yellow. The females are colorless, but they have a yellow spot and a tail. These crabs will not bite you with their little pincers.

SHELL HOME

Look carefully at a mussel shell. You will see lots of tiny pea crabs attached to the shell. They eat waste from the mussel.

26

SAND SNORKELING

The masked crab hides in the sand all day. Its antennae stick up like snorkels. The males have very long pincers.

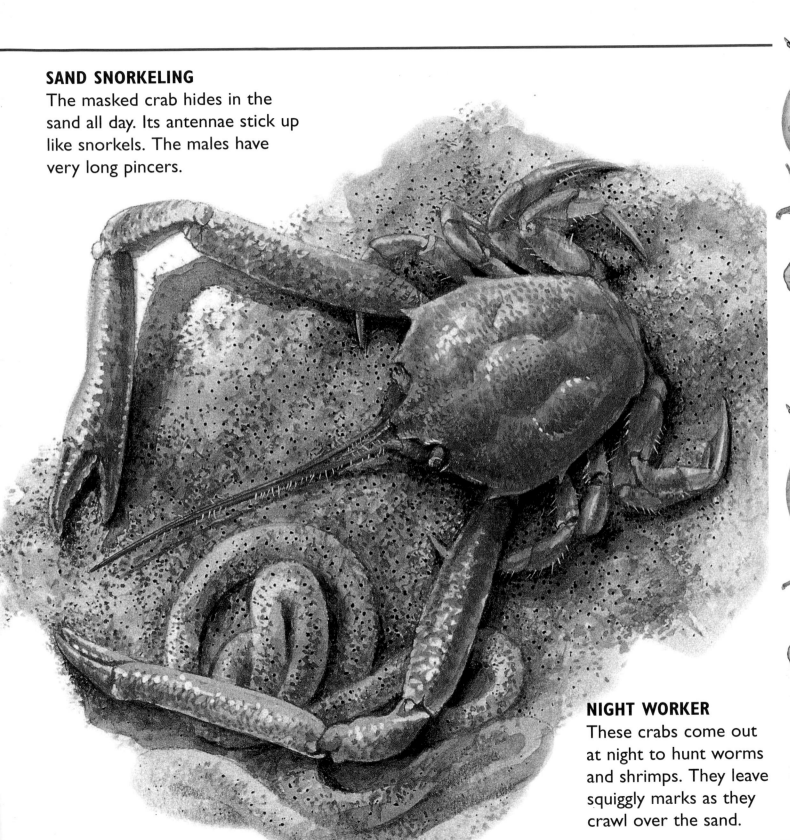

NIGHT WORKER

These crabs come out at night to hunt worms and shrimps. They leave squiggly marks as they crawl over the sand.

SEA OTTER

Sea otters live in the Pacific Ocean, off the coasts of Canada and the United States. They spend most of their lives in water. Mothers give birth to one baby at a time on the shore. Immediately, the mother carries her baby to the sea. She floats on her back, and the baby sits on her chest.

WATERY HUNT

To catch fish and collect crabs and mussels, otters dive down over 100 feet.

ALL-WEATHER COAT

Two thick layers of fur keep the otter warm. Water rolls off the fur so the otter's body is never wet.

USEFUL END

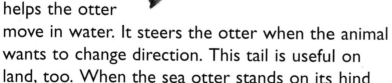

The sea otter has a short, stout tail. It is strong and helps the otter move in water. It steers the otter when the animal wants to change direction. This tail is useful on land, too. When the sea otter stands on its hind legs, the tail becomes a third leg! It helps the otter keep its balance while standing.

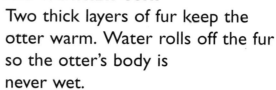

Hundreds of sea otters live together in groups called pods. They don't move far from their favorite eating, hunting, and sleeping places. They spend much of their time floating on their back. Often, they rest on large beds of kelp, a kind of floating seaweed. Otters wrap themselves in a strand of kelp so they don't float away on a wave or current. When mothers go hunting for food, they leave their babies safely in these kelp beds.

MANY CALLS

Sea otters make a barking sound. They have calls to warn other otters. The young have a special call for their mothers.

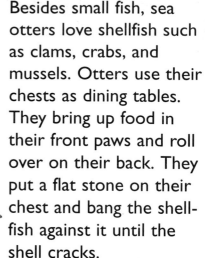

PRIVATE TABLES

Besides small fish, sea otters love shellfish such as clams, crabs, and mussels. Otters use their chests as dining tables. They bring up food in their front paws and roll over on their back. They put a flat stone on their chest and bang the shellfish against it until the shell cracks.

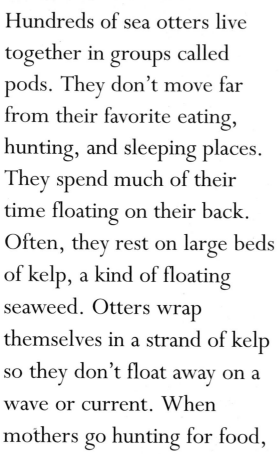

POWERFUL PAWS
The back feet have long, webbed toes with strong, flat claws.

REST PLACES
In the summer, sea otters rest on kelp beds. When winter storms wash away the kelp, otters come to shore to rest on rocks.

INDEX

GLOSSARY

Burrow - The tunnel or hole dug by an animal for its home.

Camouflage - Many animals blend with the color of the place where they live. This is called camouflage. Camouflage protects an animal from its enemies and hides it when it is trying to catch other animals.

Carnivore - An animal that eats meat is a carnivore.

Colony - A large group of animals of the same kind living together is called a colony. They build their nests or dens in one shared place.

Dorsal fin - The fin on the back of sea animals.

Fluke - A whale's tail is called a fluke.

Mammal - An animal that does not lay eggs but gives birth to its young. It also feeds its babies with milk from its breast.

Migrate - To travel, usually when the seasons change.

Mussel - A kind of shellfish that looks like a clam.

Scavenger - An animal that does not hunt for its food but eats what other animals have killed.